EXPLORING THE STATES

Kansas

THE SUNFLOWER STATE

by Blake Hoena

BELLWETHER MEDIA · MINNEAPOLIS, MN

Note to Librarians, Teachers, and Parents:

Blastoff! Readers are carefully developed by literacy experts and combine standards-based content with developmentally appropriate text.

Level 1 provides the most support through repetition of high-frequency words, light text, predictable sentence patterns, and strong visual support.

Level 2 offers early readers a bit more challenge through varied simple sentences, increased text load, and less repetition of high-frequency words.

Level 3 advances early-fluent readers toward fluency through increased text and concept load, less reliance on visuals, longer sentences, and more literary language.

Level 4 builds reading stamina by providing more text per page, increased use of punctuation, greater variation in sentence patterns, and increasingly challenging vocabulary.

Level 5 encourages children to move from "learning to read" to "reading to learn" by providing even more text, varied writing styles, and less familiar topics.

Whichever book is right for your reader, Blastoff! Readers are the perfect books to build confidence and encourage a love of reading that will last a lifetime!

This edition first published in 2014 by Bellwether Media, Inc.

No part of this publication may be reproduced in whole or in part without written permission of the publisher. For information regarding permission, write to Bellwether Media, Inc., Attention: Permissions Department, 5357 Penn Avenue South, Minneapolis, MN 55419.

Library of Congress Cataloging-in-Publication Data

Kansas / by Blake Hoena.
    pages cm. – (Blastoff! readers. Exploring the states)
Includes bibliographical references and index.
Summary: "Developed by literacy experts for students in grades three through seven, this book introduces young readers to the geography and culture of Kansas"–Provided by publisher.
ISBN 978-1-62617-015-5 (hardcover : alk. paper)
1. Kansas–Juvenile literature. I. Title.
F681.3.H65 2014
978.1–dc23

2013005584

Printed in the United States of America, North Mankato, MN.

Table of Contents

Where Is Kansas?

Did you know?
Just outside the small town of Lebanon, a monument marks the geographical center of the contiguous United States.

Colorado

New Mexico

Texas

Kansas sits in the middle of the **contiguous** United States. It is sometimes called the Central State or Midway State. Kansas is shaped like a rectangle with the northeastern corner missing. The Missouri River shapes this part of the border.

4

Nebraska lies north of Kansas, and Missouri lies to the east. Oklahoma is its southern neighbor. To the west is Colorado. Topeka, the state capital, is in the northeast.

Before Europeans arrived, **Native** American tribes grew corn and hunted bison in present-day Kansas. The United States purchased this land in 1803. In the 1850s, people living in the Kansas Territory disagreed about **slavery**. The area was called "Bleeding Kansas" because of the violent fights that broke out. In 1861, Kansas became a state just before the **Civil War** began. Kansas fought with the North for the Union.

Did you know?
Kansas settlers earned the nickname "Jayhawks" during their fight against slavery. The term was inspired by the aggressive blue jay and sneaky sparrow hawk.

Kansas Timeline!

1541: Francisco Vásquez de Coronado is probably the first European to explore the Kansas region.

1803: The United States buys land that includes Kansas in the Louisiana Purchase.

1854: The Kansas Territory is established.

1861: Kansas becomes the thirty-fourth state.

1897: Amelia Earhart is born in Atchison. She later becomes the first woman to fly alone across the Atlantic Ocean.

1930s: Kansas farmers suffer through the Dust Bowl. This is a period of dry weather and whipping winds.

1939: *The Wizard of Oz* plays in movie theaters for the first time.

1952: Dwight D. Eisenhower is elected the thirty-fourth President of the United States. He grew up in Abilene.

1954: The Supreme Court case Brown v. Board of Education of Topeka takes place. Judges rule that separating students by race goes against the U.S. Constitution.

Dwight D. Eisenhower

The Wizard of Oz

Amelia Earhart

The Land

Kansas can be divided into three main land regions. Part of the **Great Plains** covers the western half of the state. Open grasslands extend across this dry, flat area. It is perfect for grazing cattle and farming.

Northeastern Kansas is an area of high **bluffs** and river valleys. Grassy plains cover the southeastern corner of the state. The ground there is too rocky to farm. The state's location in the middle of the country can bring extreme weather. Cold air blows in from the North. Winds from the South carry a dry heat. Spring and summer come with the threat of tornadoes.

fun fact !

Cheyenne Bottoms is located in the center of Kansas. It is the largest inland marsh in the United States. Hundreds of bird species visit this wetland as they travel through the country.

Kansas's Climate
average °F

spring
Low: 41°
High: 65°

summer
Low: 64°
High: 88°

fall
Low: 43°
High: 67°

winter
Low: 21°
High: 42°

Did you know?
Little House on the Prairie is a classic children's book based in Kansas. Author Laura Ingalls Wilder tells stories about the struggles of living on the Kansas prairie.

The Flint Hills

Rolling through east-central Kansas is a region of **tallgrass prairie** called the Flint Hills. Its rocky limestone base was formed millions of years ago when a shallow sea covered the area. The limestone contains flint. This hard **mineral** does not **erode** easily. It creates a thin, rocky soil that cannot be plowed.

Most tallgrass prairies have given way to farming. The Flint Hills are home to one of the few that remain in North America. More than 80 native grass species bend and sway beneath the open sky. Other wildlife brings flashes of color to the landscape. Yellow prairie coneflowers stand tall among the grasses. Butterflies flit toward clusters of rose verbena. Dozens of birds send their songs across the prairie.

Wildlife

Kansas is known as the Sunflower State. It is home to more than ten kinds of sunflowers. Wild daisies, Indian blankets, and columbines also brighten the state's prairies. Much of Kansas is covered in open grasslands. About 200 types of grasses grow there.

Many small animals roam through Kansas. Rabbits, skunks, and prairie dogs scurry across the grasslands. Lizards and snakes dart through the state's drier areas. Kansas is home to a wide variety of birds, especially those that nest on the ground. These include wild turkeys, prairie chickens, and pheasants.

skunk

prairie chicken

fun fact !

Kansas's state tree is the cottonwood. It is sometimes called the pioneer tree. Early settlers used it to build and heat their homes.

prairie
dog

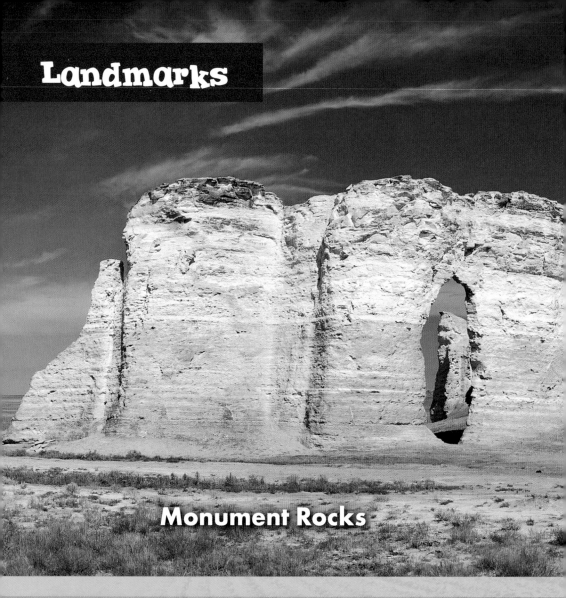

Monument Rocks

The Tallgrass Prairie National Preserve lies in eastern Kansas. This park protects one of the last regions of tallgrass prairie in North America. This type of prairie once covered large areas of the country. The park is home to a herd of American buffalo. It also boasts miles of nature trails for visitors to explore.

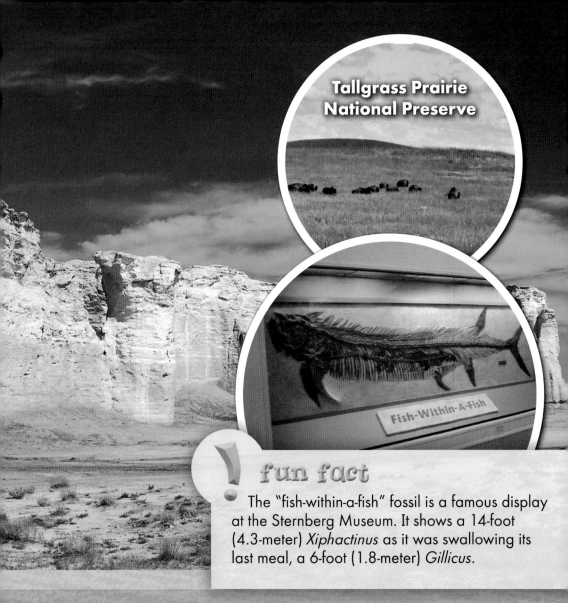

Tallgrass Prairie National Preserve

Fish-Within-A-Fish

fun fact

The "fish-within-a-fish" fossil is a famous display at the Sternberg Museum. It shows a 14-foot (4.3-meter) *Xiphactinus* as it was swallowing its last meal, a 6-foot (1.8-meter) *Gillicus*.

In western Kansas, Monument Rocks and Castle Rock tower above the dry plains. The soil and rock around these landmarks have eroded. Rocky **spires** remain. The erosion has exposed many **fossils**. The ancient remains of fish, turtles, sharks, and flying reptiles rest here. They can be seen up close at the Sternberg Museum of Natural History in Hays.

Dodge City

Dodge City, in western Kansas, is a picture of the Old Wild West. The small town was founded in the late 1800s as railroads first reached the area. Cowboys would drive their cattle into town so railroad cars could haul them off to market.

After the hard work was done, the cowboys stayed to celebrate. Gunfights often broke out, and people were killed. Lawmen like Wyatt Earp and Bat Masterson tried to control the Wild West. Today, people can stroll down a **replica** of the old Dodge City Front Street. Visitors discover what life was like in those **unruly** times.

Front Street replica

fun fact

Near the center of Dodge City is a cemetery called Boot Hill. Many of the cowboys buried there were still wearing their boots. If a cowboy "died with his boots on," it meant that he died in a gunfight.

Did you know?

A small part of the Hutchinson salt mine is home to government documents and Hollywood film reels. Its cool, dry air protects these important items from damage.

The flat, open prairies of Kansas make it a major farming state. More wheat is grown here than in any other state. Sunflowers, corn, and soybeans are other important crops. Workers on farms and ranches raise beef cattle, dairy cattle, and hogs.

Mining and **manufacturing** are also important to the state. The ancient seas that once covered Kansas left behind several large salt mines. Natural gas and oil wells dot the west. Factory workers process meat and grains from the state's farms. Kansas is also a leading producer of aircraft.

Where People Work in Kansas

manufacturing
10%

farming and
natural resources
5%

government
16%

services
69%

Playing

Kansans love activities that celebrate the state's farming culture. At **rodeos**, cowboys and cowgirls perform in roping and riding competitions. Farmers carve mazes out of cornfields and take people on hayrides. In the fall, they invite guests to pick bright orange pumpkins from their pumpkin patches.

Kansans are fierce fans of their college basketball teams. The University of Kansas Jayhawks basketball team was founded in 1898. It is nearly as old as the sport itself. The Jayhawks men's team has won three national championships.

fun fact !

Dr. James Naismith was the inventor of basketball. He founded the University of Kansas basketball team in 1898.

Jayhawks

Bierocks

Ingredients:

3 cups chopped cabbage

1 cup chopped onion

1/2 pound ground beef

1 tablespoon salt

1/2 teaspoon pepper

1 cup sharp cheese

Bread dough or biscuit dough

Directions:

1. Brown ground beef and season with salt and pepper. Add onions and cabbage. Cover and cook about 15 minutes.

2. Fold in cheese and cool until lukewarm.

3. Roll dough to 1/4 inch thick and cut into squares. Put filling on each square. Pull up all edges and pinch together.

4. Place on a greased pan. Let rise 20 minutes.

5. Bake at 350°F for 20 minutes until golden brown.

barbecue ribs

! **fun fact**

Kansans munch on popcorn and sunflower seeds made in their home state. Kansas is a leading producer of both snacks.

Many foods in Kansas have a Western flair. People make spicy chili at cook-offs. Barbecue ribs are tossed on the grill and smothered in a tangy sauce. The state's wheat and other grains go into delicious homemade breads. Steak dishes are also popular. Chicken-fried steak is a piece of beef that is battered and then fried like chicken.

Many Kansans are of German heritage. Family gatherings feature foods like sausages, cabbage rolls, and *bierocks*. *Bierocks* are pastry pockets filled with beef, cabbage, and onions.

23

Festivals

Since 1913, the Kansas State Fair has honored the hard work of farming. The state's farmers show off their livestock and produce. People gather to dance and listen to music. **Vendors** serve popular treats from across the state.

Kansas holds several events to celebrate its past. **Tourists** learn about wartime life at the Civil War **Encampment** at **Fort** Scott National Historic Site. An annual Fall Festival is held at the Shawnee Indian Mission State Historic Site. Visitors can enjoy handmade crafts, **traditional** storytelling, and Native American dance performances.

Kansas State Fair

The Wizard of Oz

The Wizard of Oz movie

fun fact !

Sedan used more than 11,000 bricks to pave its yellow brick road. It is the longest yellow brick road in the world!

The Wonderful Wizard of Oz by L. Frank Baum was a book published in 1900. This famous story follows Dorothy, a young girl trying to return to her beloved home in Kansas. In 1939, the book was made into a movie.

Oz Museum

Did you know?
A popular quote from the movie says, "We're not in Kansas anymore." People now use this phrase when they are in a strange, unfamiliar place.

Today, the Oz Museum in Wamego has more than 2,000 Oz-related items. The small town of Sedan built a yellow brick road like the one in the story. *The Wonderful Wizard of Oz* is still a source of pride to the people of Kansas. Its fierce and loyal heroine reminds them that there's no place like home.

Kansas's Flag

The flag of Kansas is a field of blue with the state name across the bottom and a sunflower at the top. In the center of the flag is the state seal. It tells the story of Kansas's history. A farm scene shows that Kansas has succeeded through farming. Also on the seal are 34 stars to symbolize that Kansas was the 34th state to join the Union.

State Flower
common sunflower

State Nicknames:	The Sunflower State
	The Wheat State
	The Central State
State Motto:	*Ad Astra Per Aspera*; "To the Stars Through Difficulties"
Year of Statehood:	1861
Capital City:	Topeka
Other Major Cities:	Wichita, Overland Park, Kansas City
Population:	2,853,118 (2010)
Area:	82,278 square miles (213,099 square kilometers); Kansas is the 15th largest state.
Major Industries:	farming, manufacturing, mining, services
Natural Resources:	farmland, oil, natural gas, salt
State Government:	125 representatives; 40 senators
Federal Government:	4 representatives; 2 senators
Electoral Votes:	6

State Animal
American buffalo

State Bird
western meadowlark

29

Glossary

bluffs—cliffs or steep banks

Civil War—a war between the northern (Union) and southern (Confederate) states that lasted from 1861 to 1865

contiguous—connected by common borders; the contiguous United States includes every state except Alaska and Hawaii.

encampment—a place where troops set up a temporary shelter or camp

erode—to wear away

fort—a strong building made to protect lands; forts are often occupied by troops and surrounded by other defenses.

fossils—the remains of ancient plants or animals that have been preserved in rock

Great Plains—a region of flat or gently rolling land in the central United States; the Great Plains stretch over about one-third of the country.

manufacturing—a field of work in which people use machines to make products

mineral—a natural substance found in the earth

native—originally from a specific place

replica—an exact copy

rodeos—events where people compete at tasks such as bull riding and calf roping; cowboys once completed these tasks as part of their daily work.

slavery—a system in which certain people are considered property

spires—slender rock towers that come to a point

tallgrass prairie—a level or rolling land of tall grasses found in North America

tourists—people who travel to visit another place

traditional—relating to a custom, idea, or belief handed down from one generation to the next

unruly—not easily controlled or managed

vendors—people who sell goods

To Learn More

AT THE LIBRARY
Baum, L. Frank. *The Wonderful Wizard of Oz*. New York, N.Y.: Barnes & Noble, 2012.

Nault, Jennifer. *Kansas: The Sunflower State*. New York, N.Y.: Weigl, 2012.

Wilder, Laura Ingalls. *Little House on the Prairie*. New York, N.Y.: HarperFestival, 2003.

ON THE WEB
Learning more about Kansas is as easy as 1, 2, 3.

1. Go to www.factsurfer.com.

2. Enter "Kansas" into the search box.

3. Click the "Surf" button and you will see a list of related Web sites.

With factsurfer.com, finding more information is just a click away.

Index

The images in this book are reproduced through the courtesy of: Phant, front cover; North Wind Picture Archives/ Alamy, p. 6; (Collection)/ Prints & Photographs Division/ Library of Congress, p. 7 (left, right); Everett Collection/ Glow Images, p. 7 (middle); George Ostertag/ SuperStock, p. 8; Orville Courtney/ Courtney Legacy Photography/ Getty Images, pp. 8-9; John Elk, pp. 10-11; Critterbiz, p. 12 (top); Tom Reichner, p. 12 (middle); Cantelow, p. 12 (bottom); Scott Payne, pp. 12-13; Michael Vorobiev, pp. 14-15; ricardoreitmeyer, p. 15 (top); Allen Holder/ KRT/ Newscom, p. 15 (bottom); Andre Jenny Stock Connection Worldwide/ Newscom, p. 16 (top); Robert Mayne USA/ Alamy, p. 16 (bottom); Chuck Haney/ Danita Delimont Photography/ Newscom, pp. 16-17; Keith Myers/ MCT/ Newscom, p. 18; Steve Heap, p. 19; ZUMA Press/ Alamy, p. 20; Diane Garcia, pp. 20-21; dirkr, p. 22; Brandon Bourdages, p. 23 (top); Karen Sarraga, p. 23 (bottom); Joel Sartore/ National Geographic Image Collection/ Glow Images, pp. 24-25; Everett Collection, p. 26; Olivia Blanco Mullins/ AFP/ Getty Images/ Newscom, pp. 26-27; pakmor, p. 28 (top); majeczka, p. 28 (bottom); Martha Marks, p. 29 (left); Eric Isselee, p. 29 (right).